BULLDOGS

by Diane Bailey
Dog Expert: Beth Adelman, MS
Former editor, *American Kennel Club Gazette*

Kaleidoscope
Minneapolis, MN

The Quest for Discovery Never Ends

This edition first published in 2021 by Kaleidoscope Publishing, Inc.

For information regarding permission, write to
Kaleidoscope Publishing, Inc.
6012 Blue Circle Drive
Minnetonka, MN 55343

Library of Congress Control Number
2020936235

ISBN
978-1-64519-437-8 (library bound)
978-1-64519-449-1 (ebook)

Printed in the United States of America.

Bigfoot lurks within one of the images in this book. It's up to you to find him!

TABLE OF CONTENTS

Introduction
Here Comes a Bulldog!

Jonah looked at the clock. It was almost time for Buttercup to get here! His neighbor was moving. She could not take her Bulldog to her new home. Jonah's parents said he could adopt Buttercup.

Jonah met Buttercup when she was just a puppy. He always stopped to say hi when he saw her in the hallway of his apartment building. Sometimes he fed her a little treat. He always giggled when Buttercup pushed her **muzzle** into his hand. She was very slobbery!

Now Buttercup would be all his. He could spend every day with her—just as soon as the doorbell rang.

Ding-dong!

It was time!

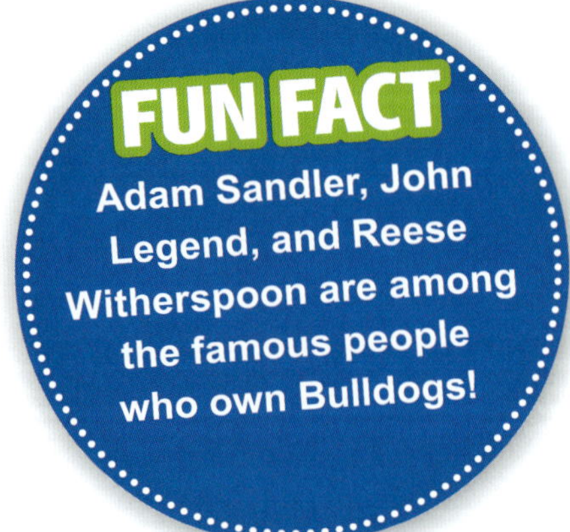

FUN FACT

Adam Sandler, John Legend, and Reese Witherspoon are among the famous people who own Bulldogs!

Chapter 1

The Story of Bulldogs

Today's Bulldogs are gentle and sweet. That was not always the case. The first Bulldogs were bred in England hundreds of years ago. Their owners wanted them to be tough. Bulldogs got their name because they were used in a sport called bull-**baiting**.

The dogs would jump on the bull and clamp their jaws on its nose. People watched these contests for entertainment.

Bulldogs were tough on bulls. But they were always good companions for their owners. They stopped fighting as soon as they were told.

Bull-baiting was cruel and dangerous for bulls and dogs. It was made illegal in 1835.

FUN FACT
Early Bulldogs were also used on farms and ranches to help **herd** cattle.

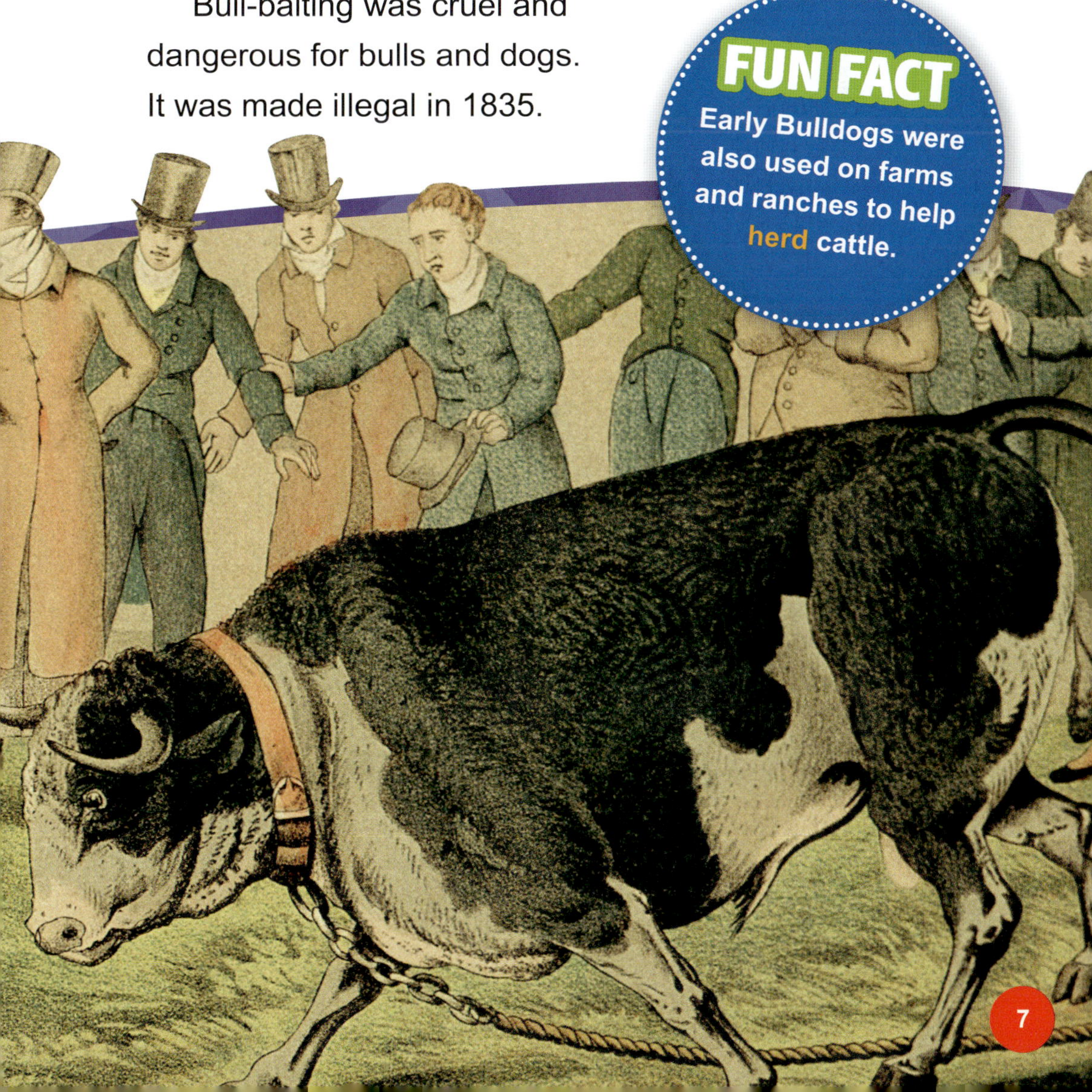

Without a job to do, Bulldogs almost became **extinct**. But some people wanted to keep the breed going. They knew that Bulldogs were great dogs, even when there was no fighting to be done. They were loyal, brave, and determined. Breeders began raising Bulldogs who still had those good qualities, but were less aggressive with other animals.

GO BULLDOGS!

Bulldogs are a popular mascot. Yale University in Connecticut was one of the first colleges to call its sports teams Bulldogs. Today, more than 15 colleges are called Bulldogs. The U.S. Marines have a Bulldog mascot, too. In Great Britain, the Bulldog's history and popularity make it the country's national dog.

Different types of dogs belong to different groups. Bulldogs are in the Non-Sporting Group. That is surprising, since their first job was part of a sport! However, today's Bulldogs have changed a lot. They are not as tall and not as long. They are also less active than early Bulldogs. Now, they mostly like to hang out with their humans and take naps.

WHERE BULLDOGS COME FROM

NORWAY

SCOTLAND

North Sea

IRELAND

ENGLAND

GERMANY

England

FRANCE

Atlantic Ocean

SPAIN

FUN FACT

Bulldogs began coming to the Americas in the 1600s.

Chapter 2
Looking at a Bulldog

Buttercup gets a lot of attention when Jonah takes her to the park. People love to pet her. There is something about her that people cannot resist.

FUN FACT
A Bulldog's head is larger around than the dog is tall!

Maybe it is her short, heavy legs. Her walk looks more like a waddle! Maybe it is those droopy eyes and wrinkly face. She looks a little sad even when she is perfectly content. Or maybe it is that flat, pushed-up nose that Bulldogs are famous for. It is ugly and cute at the same time!

Buttercup has a red and white coat in a patchy pattern called **piebald**. Other Bulldogs might have gray or fawn (brown) coats. Black markings are common too.

THE BULLDOG

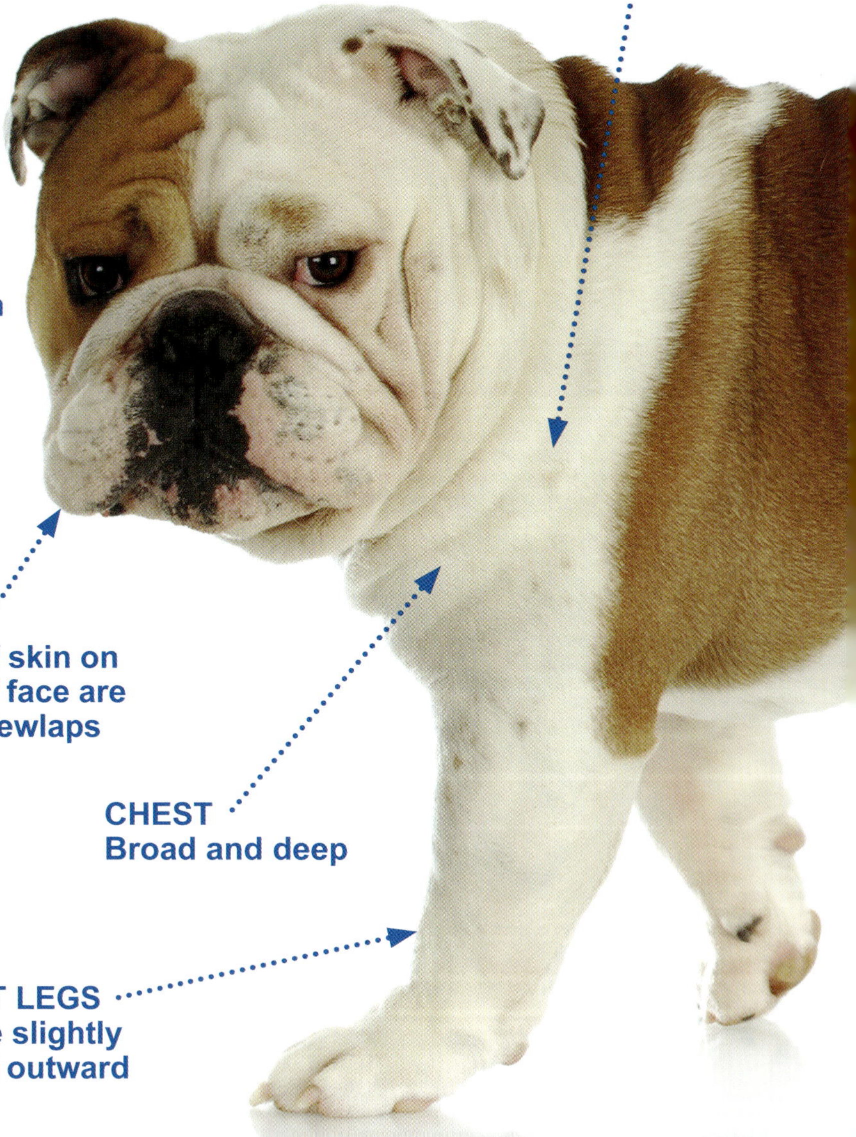

SHOULDERS
Wider than hips

FACE
Dignified expression

FACE
Flaps of skin on sides of face are called dewlaps

CHEST
Broad and deep

FRONT LEGS
Can be slightly bowed outward

MALES AND FEMALES

HEIGHT*:
14–15 in. (36–38 cm)

WEIGHT:
40–50 lbs. (18–22 kg)

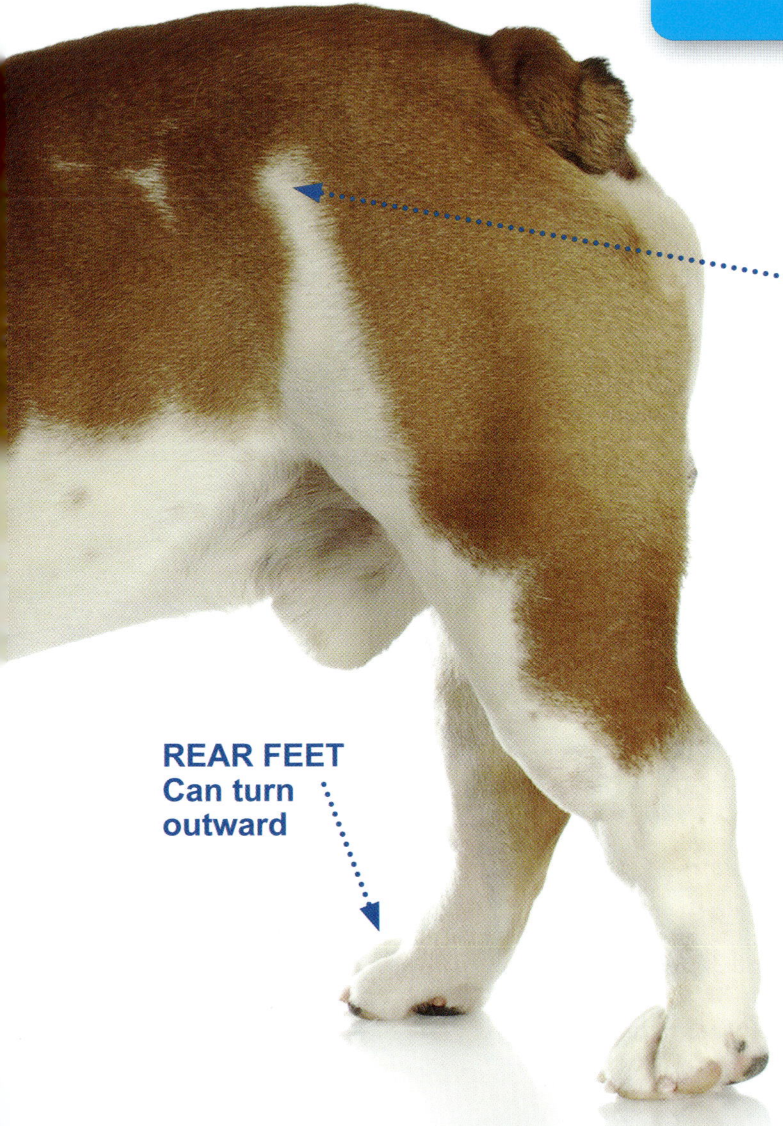

SKIN
Hangs loose on body

REAR FEET
Can turn outward

**The height of a dog is measured from the top of the shoulder, not from the top of the head.*

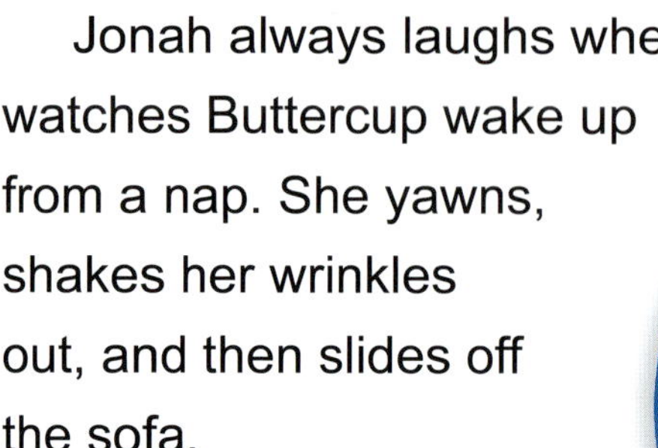

Jonah always laughs when he watches Buttercup wake up from a nap. She yawns, shakes her wrinkles out, and then slides off the sofa.

FUN FACT

A Bulldog named Thor beat 2,000 dogs to take home the Best in Show title at the National Dog Show in 2019.

Buttercup looks like a fire hydrant—strong and solid. But she is very flexible. The way she moves sometimes makes Jonah think of a bendy toy. Her legs can stretch far out to either side. She can put her neck flat on the floor. Her loose skin flaps around her. She looks like a puddle made out of dog!

Chapter 3

Meet a Bulldog!

Buttercup is an easygoing dog. When Jonah has his friends over, they can get pretty loud. Buttercup doesn't mind. If they are having fun, she joins in. If not, she just goes back to snoring!

Kids are her favorite kind of people. She loves attention, and they love to give it to her. They rub her belly and scratch behind her ears.

One time, Jonah's friend let Buttercup chew on his cap. It must have tasted good, because she would not give it back! Bulldogs are known for being determined. That's the same quality they needed as fighting dogs. When Buttercup wants something, she digs in until she gets it!

When they feel like it, Bulldogs can be very athletic. They can run as fast as people, leap through hoops, and balance on see-saws. Some have even been trained to do human sports, like skateboarding!

Today, Buttercup is fast asleep on the sofa. Jonah nudges her to wake up. He wants to go outside. Buttercup opens one eye and looks at him lazily. She seems to say, *Why bother? I'm comfortable where I am!*

Like other Bulldogs, Buttercup does not like to be active all day. But it is still important for her to get some exercise. Jonah knows a good trick to get her moving. He jangles her leash. "Come on, Buttercup!" he says. "Let's go for a walk!"

Buttercup recognizes that word. She scrambles to her feet. A walk with Jonah can be a lot of fun—and there is a treat for her when they get home!

PUPPY TIME!

When Buttercup was a puppy, she was super cute! Bulldog puppies need lots of care. They love to chew everything. Make sure your home is ready for a puppy if you get a Bulldog.

Chapter 4
Caring for a Bulldog

Fifteen minutes is a good walk for Buttercup. Being outside for too long can be hard on her, especially in the summer. Her thick body holds in too much heat. That is very dangerous for her. The **veterinarian** has warned them to keep her inside if the weather is very hot. It's a good thing Jonah's apartment has air conditioning.

Most dogs love the water, but not Bulldogs. They carry most of their weight in the front of their bodies. Their large heads and muscular chests are heavy. That weight can pull them under the water.

Jonah makes sure to keep Buttercup clean. He brushes her coat every few days. Then he uses a damp washcloth to wipe down her skin. He doesn't want dirt and drool to collect in the loose folds of her skin. That can make her uncomfortable. He pays special attention to the wrinkles on her face.

Even though Buttercup likes treats, Jonah only gives her one each day. Bulldogs like to eat. It's easy for them to eat too much. Jonah wants to keep Buttercup trim and healthy.

BOWLED OVER

The short muzzles of Bulldogs make it hard for them to eat out of regular food bowls. They have trouble getting their faces all the way in. A good bowl for a Bulldog is one that sits at an angle on a small stand. These are easier to reach.

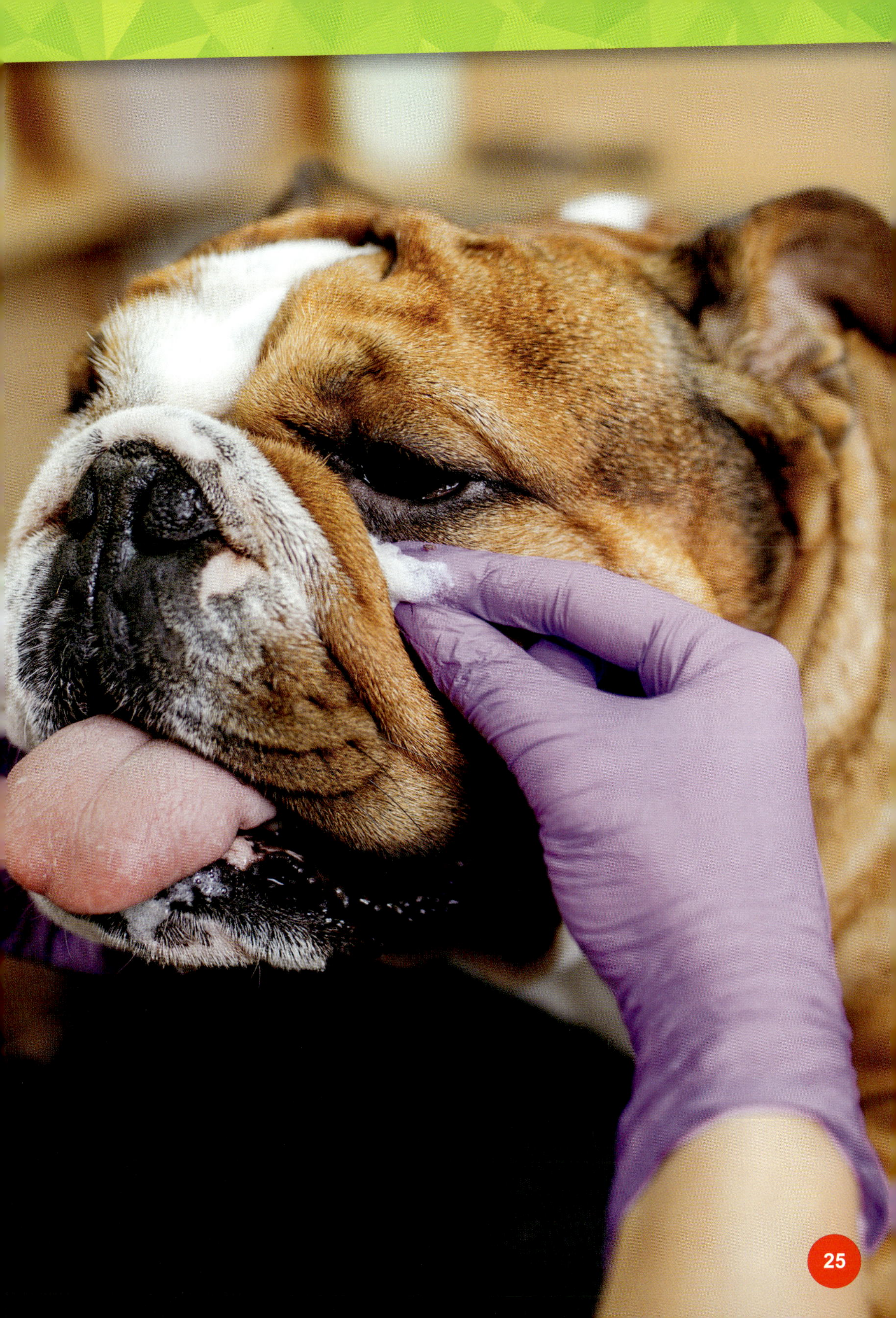

FUN FACT
Bulldogs live an average of eight to ten years.

After she is fed and groomed, Buttercup likes to lick Jonah's hands as a thank-you. Then she climbs into his lap and falls asleep. It's been a good day.

Taking good care of a Bulldog requires time and attention, since they can have more health problems than other dogs. It's important for their humans to keep an eye on things to keep them healthy.

Jonah doesn't mind doing whatever Buttercup needs. He wants to make her happy—just like she makes him happy!

BEYOND THE BOOK

After reading the book, it's time to think about what you learned. Try the following exercises to jumpstart your ideas.

RESEARCH

FIND OUT MORE. There is so much more to find out about Bulldogs. Visit the American Kennel Club's site to research Bulldogs. Or look for a Bulldog Club in your area. You can meet other people who love your favorite breed!

CREATE

TIME FOR ART. Many types of dogs are mascots for sports teams. Bulldogs are one of the most popular mascots. Pretend you are starting a new team called Bulldogs. What will your Bulldog logo look like? What sort of lettering will you use? Will the dog look friendly or fierce? Look at other dog mascot logos for inspiration.

DISCOVER

LOTS OF BREEDS. This book is about your favorite dog breed. But there are hundreds more around the world. Visit the AKC site or those of other dog organizations. What other breeds can you discover? Which breeds are related to your favorite? What is the most interesting new breed you have discovered?

GROW

HELP OUT! Animal shelters can be great places to volunteer. Contact a shelter near you and find out if you can help. Or can your family donate food or gear to help rescue dogs? Find out why dogs end up in shelters. Is there anything you can do to help them find homes?

RESEARCH NINJA

Visit www.ninjaresearcher.com/4378 to learn how to take your research skills and book report writing to the next level!

SEARCH LIKE A PRO
Learn about how to use search engines to find useful websites.

FACT OR FAKE?
Discover how you can tell a trusted website from an untrustworthy resource.

TEXT DETECTIVE
Explore how to zero in on the information you need most.

SHOW YOUR WORK
Research responsibly—learn how to cite sources.

WRITE

GET TO THE POINT
Learn how to express your main ideas.

PLAN OF ATTACK
Learn prewriting exercises and create an outline.

DOWNLOADABLE REPORT FORMS

Further Resources

BOOKS

Adelman, Beth. *Good Dog!: Dog Care for Kids.* Mankato, Minn.: Child's World: 2014.

Gagne, Tammy. *Bulldogs, Poodles, Dalmatians, and Other Non-Sporting Dogs.* Minneapolis: Capstone, 2016.

Lajiness, Katie. *Bulldogs.* Minneapolis: Big Buddy Books, 2017.

Rustad, Martha. *Bulldogs.* Mankato, Minn.: Amicus, 2017.

WEBSITES

Factsurfer.com gives you a safe, fun way to find more information.

1. Go to www.factsurfer.com.
2. Enter "Bulldogs" into the search box and click 🔍
3. Select your book cover to see a list of related websites.

Glossary

baiting: attracting an animal to trap it.

extinct: a species that has died out entirely.

herd: to make animals move together in a certain direction.

mascot: an animal or character used as a symbol for a team or organization.

muzzle: the nose and mouth of a dog.

piebald: a pattern of white spots on a colored background.

veterinarian: a doctor for animals.

Index

PHOTO CREDITS

The images in this book are reproduced through the courtesy of: Alamy: Interfoto 6. Department of Defense: 9T. iStock: KumiKomini: 12; Mladenballnovac 17; Tomalu 19; People Images 23; Group4 Studio 24. AP Images: Fred Kfoury III/Icon Sportswire 9R. Shutterstock: Ammit Jack 4; Grigorita Ko 8; WillieCole Photography 9L, 10, 14, 21; Eric Isselee 13; MilsiArt 16; Erik Gonzalez 18; Twinkle Studios 20; Lunja 22; otphoto 26.
Cover and page 1: Eric Isselee/Shutterstock. Paw prints: Maximillian Laschon/Shutterstock.

About the Author

Diane Bailey has written more than 75 books for kids and teens, on subjects ranging from sports to science to history. She lives in Kansas, where she raised two sons, two Golden Retrievers, one hamster, one mouse, and 117 ants.